SIRTFOOD DIET

———— ❧❦❧ ————

The Complete Diet Guide with Delicious Recipes to Burn Fat, Lose Weight and Get Lean

Danielle Wilder

Table of Contents

Introduction

Why is it so difficult to lose weight and keep it off? This is a question that plagues doctors, nutritionists, and – most of all – the people who struggle with their weight every day. It's not merely a question of willpower. If it were, then the people who go on crash diets and learn to live with hunger pangs would all be skinny forever. If you've ever tried one of those diets and lost weight using it, you have willpower.

Losing weight is not about deprivation, nor is it about paying thousands of dollars to eat prepackaged, tasteless food. Those things might help you lose a few pounds in the short term, but they are not a long-term solution.

Why? Because they don't give your body what it needs to lose weight. They neglect the basics of nutrition and rely on ultra-low calorie counts or eliminating necessary food groups like carbohydrates and fats. The truth is that your body is capable of losing weight, but you need to give it what it needs. Most fad diets don't do that. They focus on deprivation instead of on fulfillment.

The good news is that there's an alternative – a diet that focuses on giving your body what it needs when it needs it. If you follow it, it will help you to lose weight and keep it off. It's called The Sirtfood Diet.

What You Will Learn in This Book

The goal of this book is to help you understand The Sirtfood Diet and what it can do to help you lose weight and feel healthy and energized. I will begin by explaining the science at the heart of The Sirtfood Diet. Following this diet activates specific proteins within your body, which are known as sirtuins. I'll explain what they are and what activating them can do for you. Sirtuins play an important role in regulating your metabolism, blood sugar, and even the aging process.

After that, I'll give you a list of many of the most popular foods that qualify as sirtfoods, and give you an explanation of the role each one can play in your body. These foods are not difficult to find – in fact, many of them are probably already a part of your diet. We'll also make a comparison of superfoods and sirtfoods: how are they similar and how do they differ? With so much competing nutritional information available, it is important to know the difference.

The next step is laying out the specifics of The Sirtfood Diet. I suspect that this diet is new to you and you will be curious to learn about it and how it works. The diet itself is very simple and consists of two basic phases. I'll explain what you need to do to conform to The Sirtfood Diet, and why I believe it is the best way to lose weight. We'll also talk about the pros and cons of The Sirtfood Diet. As you might expect, this diet has its detractors. Instead of pretending those detractors don't exist, I think it is important to look at their criticisms head-on and talk about them.

Finally, the last chapter of the book will provide you with 20 simple, delicious recipes that will make it easy for you to incorporate sirtfoods into your diet starting immediately. I'll give you recipes for breakfast, lunch, and dinner, as well as a list of healthy sirtfood snacks to keep on hand. Snacking is the downfall of many people who want to lose weight, but if you prepare for cravings in advance, you can make sure that you have what you need to stay on track.

By the time you are finished reading this book, you will know everything you need to know about The Sirtfood Diet and how it can have a positive impact on your weight and on your overall health.

Are you ready to give your body what it needs? Let's get started!

Understanding Sirtuins

Any explanation of The Sirtfood Diet must begin with a basic understanding of the science that lies behind it. Every diet available has its own particular angle. Some claim they will help you lose weight by eliminating most carbohydrates from your diet. Others say that eating foods in certain combinations is the secret to weight loss.

The Sirtfood Diet uses chemicals that are already available in your body – compounds that are specifically designed to help jump-start your metabolism and help you lose weight – as its basis. The goal of The Sirtfood Diet is to make it possible for you to work with your body instead of working against it as most diets do.

What Are Sirtuins?

In the introduction, I told you that The Sirtfood Diet works by activating chemical compounds called *sirtuins* that occur naturally in your body. The average person knows very little, if anything, about sirtuins, so let's start there.

Sirtuins are proteins that are found in a wide range of living organisms both simple and complex. To give you an idea of how common they are, they are present in some of the simplest organisms on the planet, such as yeasts, as well as in highly complex organisms such as human beings.

The name given to sirtuins is a play on a much longer name: Silent Information Regulator 2 proteins, or SIR2 proteins. These proteins act as messengers within the body. They turn certain genes on or off, and they also play a role in repairing damage sustained by your DNA. The reason sirtuins are often associated with aging is that the risk of DNA damage increases as we age. Sirtuins play a role in metabolism. One school of thought is that our bodies may sometimes forget which genes need to be activated, and that sirtuins can help activate those genes and regulate metabolism.

Mammals, including humans, possess seven different sirtuins, which are numbered as SIRT1 through SIRT7.

What Role Do Sirtuins Play in the Body?

Now let's take a closer look at the specific roles that sirtuins play in the body. The original research into the role of sirtuins happened in 2003, and was conducted by David Sinclair at Harvard University. He published study results that said that the compound resveratrol, which is found in many fruits and vegetables, works to activate sirtuin in the body and trigger its anti-aging and weight loss effects.

Research has shown that overexpression of one gene, SIRT6, lengthened the lives of male mice by as much as 15.8% in a 2012 Israeli study. Humans also have SIRT6 and the research is promising in terms of what it might do for human longevity.

Sirtuins play an important role in regulating the metabolism of both fats and glucose. The body's ability to metabolize food has a direct effect on weight gain and loss.

SIRT1 regulates insulin secretion and also plays a role in the insulin sensitivity of certain cells within the body. New research is investigating whether targeting SIRT1 might be a way of preventing the onset of type 2 diabetes.

Eating a restricted-calorie diet has been shown to trigger sirtuins and accelerate weight loss and muscle building, the combination of which can have a significant impact on your body.

In addition to its metabolic, weight loss, and longevity benefits, research also suggests that targeting sirtuins may point the way to a cure for cancer. Sirtuins play a significant role in the growth of cancer cells.

As you can see, sirtuins are undeniably important when it comes to maintaining good overall health and weight loss. Now that you understand what sirtuins do, it's time to take a look at the foods that can help to trigger them – and that's what we'll do in the next chapter.

What Are Sirtfoods?

The core of The Sirtfood Diet is eating sirtfoods. These are foods that researchers have identified as doing a good job of activating sirtuins within your body. The key to losing weight and reaping the other benefits of The Sirtfood Diet is eating a diet rich in sirtfoods. This chapter will give you a list of sirtfoods so you understand what you will be eating on your new diet.

What Foods Qualify as Sirtfoods?

The foods that qualify as sirtfoods are those that are high in sirtuin activators such as resveratrol. Here are some of the most beneficial foods to eat while on the sirtfood diet.

Blackcurrants are very high in antioxidants called anthocyanins, which are found in many fruits and have been proven to help prevent heart attacks, strokes, diabetes, and heart failure. While all currants have anthocyanins, blackcurrants are the best source of sirtuin activators.

Green tea is one of the world's most popular beverages, and with good reason. The health benefits of drinking it are profound. It is a rich source of antioxidants known as catechins. It also contains Vitamin B, magnesium, folate, manganese, and potassium. Various studies have shown that drinking green tea can help with weight loss, fight cardiovascular disease, and even protect against cancer and Alzheimer's disease.

What Are Sirtfoods?

Blueberries are one of the world's richest sources of resveratrol, which has been heavily researched as a sirtuin activator. They are also rich in other vitamins and minerals. It is important to note that eating blueberries raw is the best way to have them. Heat can kill the beneficial qualities of the fruit.

Dark chocolate – identified as chocolate that contains at least 70% cacao – is very good for your health. It is rich in antioxidants, and eating small amounts every day has been shown to be beneficial in terms of reducing blood pressure and the risk of heart attacks. It is important to eat only a small amount due to its high sugar and fat content, but eating an ounce or so a day is very beneficial.

Kale is a very popular health food right now, and with good reason. It is one of the most vitamin-rich greens available. It is also high in various polyphenolic flavonoids, which are antioxidants, including beta-carotene, lutein, and zea-xanthin.

Passionfruit is one of the best dietary sources of a phytochemical known as piceatannol. To reap the benefits, it is important to eat fresh passionfruit, including the seeds. The seeds are the richest source of piceatannol.

Extra virgin olive oil and olives are a wonderful source of heart-healthy monounsaturated fat. They are rich in vitamins and amino acids, and they are also high in minerals, including iodine, iron, magnesium, potassium, and phosphorus. While their high calorie count means you need to control your intake, eating olives or olive oil can help to lower your blood pressure and cholesterol.

Parsley is arguably the world's most popular herb, and it is also a wonderfully healthy thing to include in your diet. It is one of the richest sources available of Vitamin K, which helps prevent age-related bone damage. It is also a good source of flavonoids including apigenin, apiin, crisoeriol, and luteolin; as well as containing volatile oil components including alpha-thujene, eugenol, limonene, and myristicin.

Capers are sometimes referred to as berries, but they are actually the flower buds of the Capparis shrub. The buds are typically preserved in brine and they pack a powerful punch of flavor. They are very high in the bioflavonoids quercetin and rutin. Rutin is important because it protects the small blood vessels known as capillaries, and may also help to prevent the formation of blood clots that can lead to blockages, heart attacks, and strokes. Capers are also good sources of Vitamin A, Vitamin K, niacin, and riboflavin.

Omega-3 fatty acid is a heart-healthy essential fat that is most often found in cold-water fish such as salmon and mackerel. Vegetarian sources include flaxseeds and nuts. Many people take Omega-3 as a supplement, but eating several servings of fish per week can get you what you need.

Onions are one of the best available sources of the mineral chromium, which is important since chromium plays a vital role in regulating blood sugar levels and preventing diabetes. While things like garlic tend to get a lot of attention, onions are actually a better source of polyphenols than garlic. They contain a variety of organic sulfur compounds that are very beneficial. While all onions are good for you, red onions eaten raw are the highest in sirtuin activators.

Turmeric is one of the world's most powerful antioxidants and anti-inflammatories thanks to the curcumin it contains. Many people take curcumin as a dietary supplement, but thanks to its mild flavor it can be added directly to food, too. It has been shown to help with inflammatory diseases such as arthritis. It also strengthens the liver, protects the stomach and kidneys, and may help to protect the brain against Alzheimer's disease. (People in countries where turmeric consumption is high, such as India, have significantly lower rates of Alzheimer's than countries where consumption is not as high.)

Tofu (soy bean curd) is a rich source of isoflavones, which have been shown to activate sirtuins. It is best to eat tofu with foods that contain inulin, which help to boost the body's ability to absorb isoflavones. Some good choices include asparagus and onions.

These are some of the most beneficial sirtfoods, but there are a few others you should keep in mind moving forward:

- Apples
- Coffee
- Red wine
- Buckwheat
- Celery
- Chilies
- Citrus fruits
- Lovage
- Medjool dates
- Red chicory
- Arugula
- Strawberries
- Walnuts

All of these foods, when included in your diet and eaten as part of a low-calorie regimen, can help to boost your body's sirtuin activity, and help you lose weight.

At this point, you may be wondering what the difference is between so-called superfoods and sirtfoods. We will talk about that next.

Sirtfoods vs. Superfoods: A Comparison

If you have been doing any reading about health and nutrition in recent years, you have probably heard something about superfoods. These are foods that are touted as the healthiest foods to eat.

As you read through the previous chapter, you may have noticed that some of the foods that appeared on the list of sirtfoods are also considered to be superfoods. And you may be wondering what the difference is. Why are some foods considered sirtfoods while others are not?

What Makes Sirtfoods Special

Sirtfoods and superfoods are not the same thing. A sirtfood is a food that contains any one of a number of compounds that have a specific role in the body, activating sirtuins that can help to slow the aging process, increase metabolism, and have a variety of other health benefits. Any food that does not contain one of these substances is not considered a sirtfood.

What that means in practical terms is that a food may be healthy and still not qualify as a sirtfood. For example, you may have noticed that the only animal protein that appeared on the list of sirtfoods in the previous chapter was cold-water fish, the kind that is a rich source of heart-healthy Omega 3 essential fatty acid.

Does that means that things like lean chicken or eggs are unhealthy? The answer is no. They are healthy, they are just not sirtfoods.

The same goes for many fruits and vegetables. There are many healthy foods that can be part of your diet, but they do not contain the specific things that help to activate sirtuins. For example, spinach is widely considered to be a superfood, but it is not a sirtfood. That takes nothing away from the health benefits of spinach, but it does serve to differentiate it from kale, which is a sirtfood.

It might be helpful to think of sirtfoods, many of which are also considered to be superfoods, as a particular kind of superfood. They are very healthy to eat, and eating them can have a profound effect on your wellbeing.

What Is the Difference between Sirtfoods and Superfoods?

Let's dig just a little deeper into the differences between sirtfoods and superfoods. What is a superfood? The definition is that a superfood is any food that contains high amounts of vitamins and minerals, particularly foods that are high in antioxidants. Blueberries are often mentioned as a superfood since they are very rich sources of vitamins and antioxidants. They also happen to be a sirtfood.

I mentioned spinach earlier. Spinach is a rich source of Vitamin A and iron, among many other essential nutrients. It is certainly a healthy food to eat, and it is known as a superfood with good reason. However, it is not a sirtfood.

In other words, the fact that a food has a high vitamin content is enough to make it a superfood, but not enough to have it qualify as a sirtfood. A superfood is rich in vitamins and minerals that can impact overall health. A sirtfood must contain at least one substance that has been shown to activate sirtuins within the body. That is the primary difference.

I hope that helps to explain the differences. In the next chapter, I will lay out the basics of The Sirtfood Diet so you can start to prepare to lose weight and slow the aging process.

Basics of the Sirtfood Diet

Now it's time to talk about how The Sirtfood Diet works. Unlike some other diet plans, this one is actually fairly simple. Once you understand the basics of the plan, you can follow it indefinitely. You don't have to spend thousands of dollars on strange and tasteless packaged foods. All of the foods you eat on this diet plan are whole and healthy.

The diet itself breaks down into two essential phases. The first phase involves counting calories pretty strictly, but it only lasts for seven days. The second phase, or maintenance phase, can be continued for as long as you want to.

The first question most people ask about The Sirtfood Diet is how much weight they can expect to lose by following it. That's a good question. As I said, the first week is a very low calorie plan, and most people who stick strictly to the diet can expect to lose about seven pounds. Not only that, they are also very likely to gain lean muscle mass, something that is very important for sustained health and weight loss.

Muscle burns more calories than fat does, so if you have a high percentage of muscle in your body your metabolism will get a natural boost without you having to do anything else. The fact that following this diet boosts sirtuins is extremely important. Although the first week may seem like a challenge due to the low calorie counts, many people who follow the plan find that their bodies adjust quickly. They find that they are satisfied by the foods they eat and lose the desire to snack between meals.

Phase One

As I said before, phase one of The Sirtfood Diet lasts for only one week. For many people, the biggest adjustment they must make when switching to this diet is a mental one. If you are accustomed to snacking throughout the day and eating whatever you want, you may find that you crave unhealthy foods. This is especially true if you have been eating a diet high in sugar and processed foods. Your body will experience some detoxification symptoms during the first few days.

If you do experience detox symptoms such as fatigue or a headache, remind yourself that your body is ridding itself of unhealthy toxins. The symptoms usually last only a couple of days. You can help speed the detoxification process along by drinking plenty of water, which will help flush toxins out of your system.

The first phase breaks down into two sections. The first lasts three days, and the second lasts four days. Let's look at each in turn.

The First Three Days

The first three days of The Sirtfood Diet involve a very strict eating plan that total only 1,000 calories (kCal) per day. That is a low calorie count, but you only have to stick to it for three days and then you will increase your calorie count and food intake. Think of the first three days as a mini-cleanse or detox.

The eating plan for the first three days is as follows:

1. Drink one cup of green sirtfood juice three times per day

2. Eat one sirtfood-rich meal once a day

That's it. It's actually very simple. The most complicated part of what you will be doing is making the juice. Because the juice contains very specific sirtfood ingredients, you will need to make your own. Juice is best consumed when it is fresh, so I recommend making the juice right before you drink it.

Here is the recipe for the green juice you will be drinking.

Sirtfood Green Juice

Ingredients:

- 2 handfuls (about 75 grams) of kale
- 1 handful (about 35 grams) of arugula
- 150 grams (2 or 3 stalks) of green celery
- ½ green apple
- ½ lemon, juiced
- 5 grams of parsley
- ½ tsp. Matcha (green tea) powder

Juice the kale, arugula, celery, apple, and parsley. Add the lemon juice. Add the Matcha powder and shake to combine.

You should end up with about 250 ml. of juice – that's about eight ounces, or one cup. Because Matcha powder contains caffeine, you may want to omit it from your last cup of juice of the day, particularly if consuming caffeine late in the day tends to disrupt your sleep.

As you can see, this recipe is very simple. If you will be away from home during the day, you can certainly double the batch and bring half with you in a glass jar with a lid. Keep the juice refrigerated to ensure that it does not lose vitamins.

There are no guidelines about when you should eat your one sirtfood-rich meal. Many people like to start the day with a mini-fast, drinking lemon water or green tea and waiting until about ten o'clock to drink their first juice. The sirtfood juice itself has very few calories, so your one meal will be a fairly large one that should keep you full for quite a while. Remember to keep your total calorie count to 1,000 calories for these three days.

The Next Four Days

After you get through the first three days, you transition to a plan that has a slightly higher calorie count, about 1,500 calories per day. Again, there are two basic components to the plan:

- Drink one cup of green sirtfood juice two times per day
- Eat two sirtfood-rich meals

The recipe for the juice stays the same, so the only real difference here is the number of times per day that you drink the juice (twice instead of three times) and the number of times you eat (twice instead of once.)

I strongly suggest that you stay away from the scale for the first seven days and weigh yourself only at the end of them. Daily fluctuations are normal, but if you stick to the plan you should see very good results within a week.

It is also important to note here that some people who have diabetes may need to have a small amount of protein with their green juice. The key is to keep the amounts small and factor them into your daily calorie counts. One example of a good thing to have with your green juice would be some egg whites, or a small portion (about three ounces) of boneless, skinless chicken breast.

One final note about phase one of The Sirtfood Diet. While red wine is a sirtfood, it is best not to consume alcohol during the first week of the plan. You can add that to your diet in controlled quantities once you are in phase two.

Phase Two

Some versions of The Sirtfood Diet say that phase two, which is also known as the maintenance phase, lasts for fourteen days. However, the truth is that this phase can go on indefinitely.

Unlike phase one, there is no calorie counting in phase two of the diet. However, the goal is to eat meals that are rich in sirtfoods. You may of course include some other ingredients in these meals, but the majority of what you eat should be the sirtfoods listed in the last chapter.

Phase two of the plan breaks down like this:

- Eat three sirtfood-rich meals per day
- Drink one glass of green sirtfood juice per day

Again, as you can see this plan is extremely simple. You may also consume sirtfood snacks during this phase of the plan. I will include a list of recommended snacks in the next chapter.

While there is no restriction on the number of calories you eat during this plan, you may want to control your calories depending on how much weight you want to lose. As long as you stick to meals that are primarily composed of sirtfoods, your calories will be controlled naturally because the foods included in the plan are healthy and low in calories. The majority of what you eat will come from fruits and vegetables, and it is very difficult to overeat when you consume a natural, plant-based diet.

If you do decide that you want to count calories during this part of the plan, it may be helpful to have some guidelines. You may have heard or read about a number called the base metabolic rate (BMR) which is the number of calories your body needs to perform basic functions such as breathing and digesting food. The number that is relevant for weight loss, though, is something called the total daily energy expenditure or TDEE. This number takes into account your BMR plus your basic activity level. In other words, the TDEE is the number of calories you would need to consume in order to maintain your current weight.

If you are interested in continuing to count calories, you can do so by calculating your TDEE at www.iifym.com/tdee-calculator. Once you have that number, you can backtrack to figure out the number of calories you want to consume to lose weight. One pound of weight is the equivalent of 3500 calories, so if you want to lose one pound per week you would need to create a daily calorie deficit of 500 calories. In other words, a person who needed 2300 calories to maintain their current weight would eat 1800 calories if they wanted to lose one pound per week.

The benefit of eating sirtfoods is that you do not need to stick strictly to the maintenance part of the plan to reap some of the benefits and lose weight. As long as you are eating a significant amount of sirtfoods, the sirtuins in your body will remain activated and you can continue to lose weight.

The information in this chapter provides a basic framework for the diet. In the next chapter, we will talk about some of the specific pros and cons of The Sirtfood Diet.

Pros and Cons of the Sirtfood Diet

As someone who wants to lose weight, you know that it's a difficult process. In many ways, the modern lifestyle is perfectly designed to make us gain weight. For example:

Many of us work sedentary jobs that keep us sitting at a desk all day long. What that means in real terms is that our TDEEs are lower than they would have been in previous eras when the majority of people did hard physical work every day. When people had to work the land or do laundry and churn butter by hand, they burned a large number of calories. Today we have machines to do many everyday tasks for us.

Food production techniques have grown increasingly sophisticated. As a result, we have access to highly processed foods with long shelf lives and a list of unreadable ingredients. These prepared and processed foods might be convenient, but they are also largely unhealthy. They contain unconscionably high amounts of sugar and salt. In many cases, they also contain trans fat, a highly inflammatory kind of fat that is detrimental to heart health, as well as chemicals and preservatives. In addition to being high in calories, many of these foods are inflammatory and cause systemic problems when we eat them in large quantities.

Speaking of quantities, our portion sizes have ballooned out of control. When we visit popular chain restaurants such as The Cheesecake Factory or Olive Garden, we're greeted with gigantic portions of unhealthy food. Unless we make a concerted effort to control what we eat, we may end up overeating and gaining weight as a result. It can be difficult to display will power when you have an "all you can eat" menu or bottomless salad and bread baskets.

In addition to these things, all of which contribute to an unhealthy lifestyle, we also are bombarded with a series of conflicting and contradictory images telling us what to eat and how we should look. On the one hand, television, movies, and magazines show us an endless parade of impossibly thin models. (When I say "impossibly thin" I mean not that some people are not naturally thin, but rather that the images are manipulated to show a degree of perfection that is simply not achievable without Photoshop.) These images saturate the media, telling us that the only way to be considered attractive or sexy is to have a thigh gap or a six pack.

We also get bombarded with countless options that promise to help us lose weight. Celebrities tout weight loss programs like Weight Watchers and Jenny Craig. Diet gurus hawk their products on late-night television and online. Magazines offer us tips to lose weight. One minute we hear that cutting out fat is the answer; the next, fat is healthy and carbohydrates are the enemy. It is impossible to keep it all straight.

On the other hand, we see a parade of commercials advertising unhealthy processed foods and fast foods. Chain restaurants are everywhere. Places like McDonald's offer sandwiches that contain enough sodium for an entire day. Supermarkets are jammed with processed foods – so much so that it can be difficult to avoid them.

It's easy to see why it can be so difficult to lose weight and keep it off. The truth is that the companies in the diet industry make much more when people's weight fluctuates than they do when it remains steady. For that reason, I think it is important to look seriously at the pros and cons of The Sirtfood Diet so you can understand what it offers. Is it a fad like so many diets, or is it the fat loss solution you've been wanting to find?

Pros and Cons of The Sirtfood Diet

As you might expect, The Sirtfood Diet has both champions and detractors. There are many who tout its health benefits and weight loss successes and encourage people to try it. And, conversely, there are those who caution against any diet that severely restricts calories or food options.

Pros of The Sirtfood Diet

First, let's look at the pros of following The Sirtfood Diet, some of which have already been covered in this book. I think it is important to reiterate them here.

Sirtfoods contain polyphenols, chemical compounds that help to activate proteins called sirtuins that occur naturally in the human body. Sirtuins have been proven to have beneficial effects on longevity in tests on mice.

The original study that led to The Sirtfood Diet examined the effects of the diet on 40 regular gym-goers, who lost, on average, seven pounds after just one week on the diet. Most diets lead to weight loss of about one to two pounds per week.

People who tried The Sirtfood Diet lost body fat and weight without losing lean muscle mass, which is essential for staying healthy and keeping your metabolism working at a high level.

The foods that are included in The Sirtfood Diet are universally considered to be healthy. Unlike some fad diets that focus on eating heavily processed food, sirtfoods are all-natural and readily available, consisting mostly of fresh fruits and vegetables. Very few nutritionists would look at the foods that are included and deem them to be unhealthy.

Unlike some diets, which may allow for no alcohol or sweets – something that can lead to binge eating or strong cravings for unhealthy foods – The Sirtfood Diet allows for small amounts of red wine and dark chocolate. This allowance may make the diet more palatable and appealing to people who are reluctant to give up drinking or dessert.

The Sirtfood Diet is specifically designed to work in the long term unlike many fad diets which are not sustainable for more than a short period of time. A person could eat sirtfoods for the rest of their life and stay healthy and strong.

As you can see, there are many very strong arguments for trying The Sirtfood Diet. Many people have seen remarkable weight loss results using The Sirtfood Diet.

Cons of The Sirtfood Diet

Now let's talk about the cons of The Sirtfood Diet. As I mentioned, this diet does have its detractors. Here are some of the things that they mention when talking about it.

The calorie restrictions for the first week are extreme and therefore some say that they are not healthy. A 35-year-old man who weighs 180 pounds and has a moderate level of activity needs about 2700 calories per day to maintain his weight. Clearly 1000 calories is very low when judged in this way, and some nutritionists say that it is too low even for three days.

Because the calorie restrictions for the first week are so severe, it may be difficult to separate the effects of eating sirtfoods from the effects of eating a very low-calorie diet. The chances are that someone who ate 1000 calories' worth of pasta or bananas or hot dogs would also lose weight, simply by virtue of the fact that the calorie counts are so low.

There may be some negative side effects to eating a very low calorie diet. Some people who drastically restrict their calories find that they end up feeling lethargic or mentally fuzzy as a result. It may be difficult to work or focus during the first three days of following The Sirtfood Diet.

Another nutritional concern expressed by some is that the heavy focus on eating sirtfoods actually prevents people from eating the variety of fruits and vegetables that they need in order to be healthy. Many nutritionists advocate "eating the rainbow," meaning that they encourage people to eat a wide variety of fruits and vegetables of different colors in order to ensure that they get all of the vitamins and minerals they need.

Typically before a particular effect of a diet or supplement is widely accepted by the scientific community, multiple studies would be carried out over a period of years. The usual standards involve double-blind studies, meaning that half of the participants in the study would follow a diet plan that amounts to a placebo effect, something that would make clear which effects were the result of the diet in question and which were not. The original study that forms the basis of The Sirtfood Diet looked at only 40 people. It was not a double-blind study. Some detractors of the diet say that it is not proper to base anything on a single, small study.

These points are important to examine. Every diet, particularly those that recommend calorie and dietary restrictions, carries some risk with it. There is a reason that most diets recommend that people who follow them discuss the diet with their doctors before beginning.

How to Proceed

How can we reconcile the wonderful things people say about The Sirtfood Diet with what we hear from its detractors? It is important to keep both things in mind when we evaluate the diet.

The first thing to keep in mind is that you should talk to your doctor before starting on The Sirtfood Diet. Your doctor is in the best position to know you and your body, and to understand the potential effects that following this diet might have on your body and your health. Consulting with a doctor is especially important if you have chronic or ongoing medical conditions. Earlier, I mentioned that some people who have diabetes may need to consume lean protein when drinking the green sirtfood juice that is part of the diet.

Now let's address the issue of nutrition. The thing to keep in mind is that The Sirtfood Diet does not need to be restricted only to sirtfoods. You can choose to eat a diet that is rich in sirtfoods and still supplement it with other healthy foods. The impact of the sirtfoods will not be diminished if you eat some spinach or a pear or a banana. If you were restricting your diet only to sirtfoods, you would get many vital nutrients, but a healthy and balanced diet that is rich in sirtfoods will have the same benefit as one that includes only sirtfoods.

The issue of the sirtfoods study that forms the basis of the diet is another one that must be addressed. It is true that a study of only 40 people is not a large one, nor is it scientifically conclusive. However, as I mentioned earlier in the book, that is not the only study into the effects of eating sirtfoods. I told you about a study that looked at SIRT6 and longevity in mice. There are many other studies that have examined sirtuins and their effects on the human body. Research is ongoing, but sirtuins have been studied for years and are continuing to be studied every day.

The low calorie count is something that requires us to be mindful, but the fact that the lowest calorie count of 1000 calories only applies for three days makes it less of an issue than it would be in a diet that recommends a very low calorie count on an ongoing basis. It is important to be aware of the effects that eating only 1000 calories per day may have on your body. If you have a tendency toward low blood sugar, you may need to space out your meals in such a way that your blood sugar does not dip dangerously low.

The bottom line is this. In my opinion, the health benefits of following The Sirtfood Diet far outweigh the risks. There are common sense answers to many of the potential problems, as outlined above. As long as you bring your common sense and practicality to the mix and make sure to listen to your own body, you can follow The Sirtfood Diet safely.

We've covered the pros and cons of the diet, and the next step is to provide you with some delicious and easy recipes that demonstrate just how simple it can be to follow this diet. That's what we'll cover in the next chapter.

Cooking with Sirtfoods

What can you eat on The Sirtfood Diet? That's a popular question, one that I get almost every time I talk about this diet. Food is an important part of life. It's more than merely sustenance. For many of us, mealtimes are family times. We look forward to sitting down with our spouses or children, and talking about our day. Meals are rituals and celebrations.

It can be daunting to think about cooking a separate meal for yourself if you share a household with other people. The good news is that the recipes included here are delicious and may very well appeal to the other people in your house. You can certainly add other healthy ingredients to make them more appealing, or serve with side dishes that do not include sirtfoods if you have children or picky eaters in your family.

From a practical standpoint, you may want to do some meal preparation in advance to make the process easy if you do have to cook for other people. For example, once you are past the first three days of the diet, you may want to cook enough food at dinner to provide you with leftovers for lunch the next day. Practical steps like that can make the process less labor-intensive.

With that in mind, let's look at some easy sirtfood recipes for breakfast, lunch, and dinner.

Breakfast Recipes

Easy Apple Pancakes

Ingredients:

- ½ c. all-purpose flour
- 1/3 c. whole oats
- 2 tsp. sugar
- 1 tsp. baking powder
- Pinch of salt
- 2 green apples
- 2 egg whites
- 1 ¼ c. 1% milk
- 2 tsp. light olive oil

1. Peel, core, and finely chop the apples.
2. In a large bowl, combine the flour, oats, sugar, baking powder, and salt.
3. Add the apples and stir until they are thoroughly coated.
4. Add the milk a little bit at a time, stirring until it forms a smooth batter.
5. In a separate bowl, whip the egg whites until they form stiff peaks.
6. Using a rubber spatula, fold the egg whites into the batter until combined.

7. Heat ½ tsp. of the oil in a skillet or on a griddle. Pour ¼ of the batter into the pan and cook until bubbles form on the surface. Flip the pancake once and cook for 2-3 minutes, or until cooked through.

Serve these pancakes with a quick blackcurrant compote. To make it, combine:

- ½ c. ripe blackcurrants
- 3 Tbsp. water
- 2 Tbsp. sugar

Place all items in a pot and bring to a boil. Cook until the currants burst and the compote thickens, about 10-15 minutes.

Dark Chocolate Granola

Ingredients:

- 1 c. whole oats
- ¼ c. raw walnuts, chopped
- ¼ c. good quality dark chocolate chips (at least 70% cacao)
- 3 Tbsp. light olive oil
- 2 Tbsp. rice malt syrup
- 1 Tbsp. brown sugar
- 1 Tbsp. butter

1. Preheat the oven to 325 degrees.
2. Line a cookie sheet with parchment paper or silicone sheet.
3. Mix the oats and walnuts in a large bowl.
4. In a small pot, combine the olive oil, malt syrup, brown sugar, and butter. Heat over medium heat until the sugar has dissolved and the butter has melted, but do not let it boil.
5. Pour the heated mixture over the oats and stir until the oats are completely coated.
6. Pour the oats onto the cookie sheet and spread them evenly. Bake them for 20 minutes, or until the oats turn golden brown around the edges.
7. Allow to cool thoroughly.

8. Use your fingers to break up the granola, then mix in the chocolate chips and transfer to an air-tight jar.

This granola will keep for up to two weeks as long as you store it properly.

Sirtfood Fruit Salad

Ingredients:

- 1 medium green apple, cored and roughly chopped
- 1 orange, cut in half
- 10 red grapes
- 10 blueberries
- ½ c. freshly brewed green tea
- 1 tsp. raw honey

1. Combine the apple, grapes, and blueberries in a bowl.
2. Squeeze the juice of one half of the orange into the fruit.
3. Chop the other half of the orange and add the fruit to the bowl.
4. Stir the honey into the green tea and allow it to dissolve.
5. Pour the tea over the fruit, and enjoy immediately.

Blackcurrant and Kale Breakfast Smoothie

Ingredients:

- 1 ripe banana
- ¼ c. blackcurrants
- 10 baby kale leaves, stems removed
- 1 c. freshly made green tea
- 2 tsp. honey
- 6 ice cubes

1. Stir the honey into the warm green tea until it is completely dissolved.
2. Add all ingredients to the blender and blend until smooth.

This recipe is easy to double if you have more than one person in your family doing The Sirtfood Diet.

Green Sirtfood Omelet

Ingredients:

- 2 large eggs at room temperature
- 1 handful of arugula
- 2 Tbsp. chopped flat leaf parsley
- 1 Tbsp. chopped red onion
- 1 Tbsp. olive oil

1. Put the olive oil into a large frying pan and heat it gently.
2. Add the onion and cook over low heat for approximately five minutes, or until the onion is translucent.
3. Beat the two eggs in a bowl.
4. Spread the onions out evenly over the pan before pouring the eggs into the pan.
5. Cook for one or two minutes until the eggs begin to set at the edges, then lift the edges, and let the uncooked eggs run underneath the cooked eggs.
6. Add the arugula and parsley to the top of the eggs.
7. Continue cooking until the eggs are nearly set. Fold the omelet in half and continue cooking for one more minute.
8. Transfer to a plate and enjoy.

Blackcurrant Yogurt Parfait

Ingredients:

- 1 c. natural yogurt (Greek yogurt is acceptable)
- ½ c. blackcurrants
- ½ c. water
- ¼ c. whole oats
- 1 tsp. sugar

1. Preheat the oven to 350 degrees.

2. Spread the oats onto a lined cookie sheet and bake until they are lightly golden brown, or about 15 minutes. Allow to cool.

3. In a small pot, combine the blackcurrants and sugar. Bring to a boil and cook for about five minutes, or until the compote thickens. Remove from the heat.

4. In a cup, alternate layers of yogurt, oats, and blackcurrant compote.

5. Garnish with whole blackcurrants and serve immediately.

These six breakfast recipes are all extremely easy to make and can be easily amended to incorporate other ingredients. For example, you could make the parfait with blueberries instead of blackcurrants.

Lunch Recipes

Shrimp Stir Fry with Buckwheat Noodles

Ingredients:

- 5 oz. shrimp, shelled and deveined
- ½ c. green beans, chopped
- ½ c. kale, roughly chopped
- 1/3 c. celery, chopped
- 1 chili (jalapeño or bird's-eye), chopped and seeded
- ¼ c. chicken stock
- 1 garlic clove, minced
- 1 Tbsp. red onion, chopped
- 2 tsp. soy sauce or tamari
- 2 tsp. olive oil
- 1 tsp. finely chopped fresh ginger
- 1 tsp. lovage or celery leaves, chopped

1. In a wok or large skillet, cook the shrimp in one teaspoon of the oil and one teaspoon of the soy sauce or tamari. Cook until they are just opaque, then remove to a place and wipe out the pan.

2. Cook the buckwheat noodles per the package instructions. When they are cooked, drain them and put them in a bowl.

3. Put the remaining oil and soy sauce in the wok or skillet. Add the green beans, kale, celery, chili, red onion, garlic and ginger. Cook until the green beans are crisp-tender, about four to five minutes.

4. Add the shrimp, noodles, and chicken stock to the pan and stir until everything is combined.

5. Remove from heat and serve, sprinkling the lovage or celery leaves over the top.

Aromatic Chicken Salad

Ingredients:

- 4 ounces boneless, skinless chicken breast
- 2 c. baby kale, stems removed
- ½ c. cherry tomatoes
- ¼ c. blueberries
- ¼ c. chopped red onion
- ½ tsp. turmeric
- 1 tsp. light olive oil
- Salt and pepper to taste

1. Pound out the chicken breast until it has an even thickness.
2. Sprinkle the chicken with turmeric, salt, and pepper on both sides.
3. Heat the olive oil in a skillet over medium heat.
4. Cook the chicken breast for four minutes, then flip and cook for another three or four minutes or until cooked through. Remove from the pan.
5. In a large bowl, combine the kale, tomatoes, blueberries, and red onions.
6. Slice the chicken and add it to the bowl.

Top with a simple dressing made with extra virgin olive oil and lemon juice.

Spinach and Salmon Wraps

Ingredients:

- 4 ounces salmon
- 2 handfuls baby spinach leaves
- 1 handful baby kale, stems removed
- 1 buckwheat wrap
- 2 tsp. light olive oil, divided
- 1 tsp. prepared Dijon mustard.

1. Heat one teaspoon of the olive oil in a skillet.
2. Add the salmon and cook until the fish easily releases from the pan. Flip the fish and continue cooking to the desired degree of doneness. Remove to a plate and allow to cool.
3. Spread out the buckwheat wrap and top with the baby spinach and kale.
4. Using a fork, shred the salmon and put it on top of the greens.
5. In a small bowl, whisk together the olive oil and the Dijon mustard until it makes a smooth vinaigrette.
6. Drizzle the vinaigrette over the salmon.
7. Roll the buckwheat wrap carefully, securing with a toothpick.
8. Cut the wrap in half and serve immediately.

If you will be away from home, you may want to transport the wrap ingredients separately and assemble them when you are ready to eat.

Greek Salad Skewers

Ingredients:

- 2 wooden skewers
- 8 large olives, pitted
- 8 cherry tomatoes
- 1 yellow pepper, seeded and cut into 8 pieces
- ½ red onion, cut into 8 pieces
- 8 slices of cucumber
- 8 1-inch cubes of feta cheese
- 1 Tbsp. extra virgin olive oil
- 1 Tbsp. fresh squeezed lemon juice
- 1 tsp. aged balsamic vinegar
- 1 tsp. fresh oregano, chopped
- Salt & pepper to taste

1. Thread the ingredients onto the skewers, alternating as follows: olive, tomato, pepper, onion, cucumber, and feta cheese. You should end up with two of each item on each skewer.

2. In a small bowl, combine the olive oil, lemon juice, balsamic vinegar, oregano, salt, and pepper until completely mixed.

3. Drizzle the dressing over the skewers and serve immediately.

If you feel you need a bit more protein with this lunch, you can have it with three ounces of tuna packed in water.

Open Sesame Chicken Salad

Ingredients:

- 5 ounces cooked chicken breast, chopped
- 1 handful baby kale leaves
- 1 handful mixed spring greens
- 1 cucumber, peeled, seeded, and chopped
- ¼ c. shredded bok choy
- ½ red onion, minced
- 2 Tbsp. flat leaf parsley, chopped
- 1 Tbsp. sesame seeds

Dressing:

- 1 Tbsp. olive oil
- 2 tsp. soy sauce or tamari
- Juice of one lime
- 1 tsp. honey
- 1 tsp. sesame oil

1. In a small bowl, combine all dressing ingredients and whisk until combined.

2. Heat a dry frying pan over medium heat. Add the sesame seeds and cook for about two minutes or until light brown. (Watch them carefully or they may burn). Remove them from the heat.

3. In a bowl, combine the kale, spring greens, cucumber, bok choy, red onion, and parsley.

4. Top the vegetables with the dressing and toss until combined.

5. Put the salad on a plate and top with the chicken breast.

6. Sprinkle with sesame seeds and serve.

Smoked Salmon Frittata

Ingredients:

- 2 medium eggs at room temperature
- 3 ounces smoked salmon, chopped
- 1 handful arugula, chopped
- 1 tsp. flat leaf parsley, chopped
- 1 tsp. olive oil
- ½ tsp. capers

1. Preheat the oven to 400 degrees
2. Heat the olive oil in an oven-safe skillet over medium heat.
3. Break the eggs and beat them in a medium-sized bowl.
4. Add the smoked salmon, arugula, capers, and parsley and stir until combined.
5. Pour the mixture into the pan and cook until the bottom is just set.
6. Transfer the pan to the oven and cook for about 10 minutes or until the eggs on top are just set and the frittata is cooked through.
7. Cut into wedges and serve immediately.

This frittata would also be good with other smoked fish such as trout or mackerel, both of which are also good sources of Omega 3 essential fatty acid.

Steak and Kale

Ingredients:

- 4 ounces lean steak at room temperature
- 2 handfuls baby kale, stems removed
- ½ red onion, minced
- 1 shallot, minced
- 2 tsp. olive oil, divided
- Salt and pepper to taste.

1. Heat one teaspoon of the olive oil in a large skillet over medium heat.

2. Sprinkle the steak with salt and pepper on both sides. Add to the skillet, and cook for about five minutes.

3. Flip the steak once, and continue cooking to the desired level of doneness. (1-2 minutes for medium rare, 3-4 minutes for medium, 5-6 minutes for well done.)

4. Remove the steak to a plate and let it rest while you cook the kale.

5. In the same pan, add the remaining teaspoon of olive oil. Cook the red onion for a minute or two until they have just started to soften. Add the kale and cook until wilted, about three or four minutes.

6. Put the steak on a plate. Put the kale next to it and serve immediately.

Dinner Recipes

Mushroom Dinner Scramble

Ingredients:

- 2 medium eggs at room temperature
- 1 handful baby kale, chopped
- ½ c. white button mushrooms, sliced
- ½ jalapeño pepper, seeded and chopped
- 1 Tbsp. flat leaf parsley, chopped
- 1 tsp. ground turmeric
- 1 tsp. mild curry powder
- 1 tsp. olive oil

1. In a small dish, combine the turmeric and curry powder with a little water and stir until it makes a paste.
2. Heat the olive oil in a skillet over medium-high heat.
3. Add the mushrooms, jalapeno, and turmeric-curry paste, and cook over medium heat until the mushrooms have softened and browned.
4. In a small bowl, beat the eggs. Pour them over the mushrooms and chilies.
5. Using a rubber spatula or wooden spoon, gently scramble the eggs as they cook.
6. Just before the eggs are done, add the kale and parsley, stirring to allow the heat of the eggs to wilt the greens.
7. Serve immediately. If you wish, you can serve this with lettuce leaves for wrapping, or with a buckwheat wrap.

Marinated Cod and Asparagus

Ingredients:

- 5 ounces black cod or Atlantic cod
- 4 teaspoons miso paste
- 1 Tbsp. mirin
- 1 Tbsp. extra virgin olive oil, divided
- 8 ounces asparagus
- 1 tsp. soy sauce or tamari
- 1 tsp. sesame seeds

1. Preheat the oven to 350 degrees.

2. In a small bowl, mix the miso, mirin, and one teaspoon of the olive oil. Pour the marinade over the cod and allow it to marinate for at least 30 minutes.

3. Mix one teaspoon of the olive oil with the soy sauce and pour over the asparagus. Transfer the asparagus to a lined cookie sheet or a shallow baking dish. Bake the asparagus until it just begins to brown, about 25 to 30 minutes.

4. In a skillet, heat the remaining one teaspoon of the olive oil. Remove the cod from the marinade and add it to the pan, reserving the marinade. Cook it for five minutes or until the fish separates easily from the pan and can be flipped. Turn it and continue cooking until the fish is opaque and flaky.

5. Remove the fish and add the marinade to the pan. Cook until the marinade boils, then lower the heat and continue cooking until the marinade is reduced by half.

6. Serve the cod with a drizzle of the cooked-down marinade and a sprinkle of sesame seeds. Serve the asparagus on the side.

Crispy Pork and Tofu Stir Fry

Ingredients:

- 8 ounces extra-firm tofu
- 8 ounces minced pork
- 4 ounces Shiitake mushrooms, sliced
- 4 ounces bok choy, shredded
- 4 ounces bean sprouts
- 2 Tbsp. olive oil

Ingredients for Sauce:

- 4 ounces low-sodium chicken stock
- 1 Tbsp. rice wine
- 1 Tbsp. soy sauce or tamari
- 1 Tbsp. brown sugar
- 1 Tbsp. tomato puree
- 1 Tbsp. corn flour
- 1 Tbsp. water
- 1 Tbsp. ginger, peeled and minced
- 1 clove of garlic, peeled and minced

1. Combine the corn flour and water in a small bowl and whisk until it is combined and there are no lumps.
2. Add the remaining sauce ingredients, and stir until combined.

3. Dice the tofu and pat it dry between two layers of paper towel. Allow it to sit on the paper towel until you are ready to use it.

4. Heat the olive oil in a wok. Add the Shiitake mushrooms and cook until they are brown and have begun to soften, about three minutes.

5. Remove the mushrooms and add the tofu and stir fry until it is golden brown on all sides.

6. Remove the tofu and add the bok choy and bean sprouts. Cook until just tender, then add the sauce. Add the mince and tofu back to the wok and stir to coat with the sauce. Continue cooking until just heated through. Serve immediately.

White Bean Stew

Ingredients:

- 8 ounces canned white beans, drained and rinsed
- 8 ounces low-sodium chicken stock
- 1 16-ounce can of chopped tomatoes
- 2 handfuls baby kale, stems removed
- ¼ c. buckwheat
- ½ red onion, finely chopped
- 1 stalk celery, chopped
- 1 carrot, chopped
- 1 garlic clove, minced
- 1 Tbsp. flat leaf parsley, chopped
- 1 Tbsp. extra virgin olive oil
- 1 tsp. tomato puree
- 1 tsp. Herbes de Provence

1. Place a large pot over medium heat and heat the olive oil.
2. Add the onion, celery, carrot, and garlic, and herbes de Provence, and cook them until they begin to soften.
3. Add the chicken stock, canned tomatoes, and tomato puree and bring to a boil.
4. Add the beans and simmer for about 30 minutes.
5. Separately, cook the buckwheat according to the package instructions. Drain it and set it aside.

6. Add the kale to the stew and cook until tender, about five to ten minutes.

7. Stir in the parsley at the last minute.

8. Serve the stew with the buckwheat.

Turkey Cutlets with Cauliflower "Risotto"

Ingredients:

- 6 ounces turkey cutlets
- 6 ounces cauliflower
- ½ red onion, chopped
- 1/3 c. sundried tomatoes, chopped
- 1 garlic clove, minced
- ½ lemon, juiced
- 2 Tbsp. extra virgin olive oil
- 1 Tbsp. parsley, chopped
- 1 Tbsp. capers
- 1 Tbsp. fresh ginger, chopped
- 2 tsp. ground turmeric
- 1 tsp. dried sage
- Salt and pepper to taste

1. Cut the cauliflower into florets and put it in a food processor, pulsing it until it resembles couscous.

2. Heat one teaspoon of the olive oil in a skillet. Cook the red onion, garlic, and ginger for a minute to release the aromas, then add the cauliflower and turmeric.

3. Cook the cauliflower for 2 minutes, or until just softened. Remove it from the heat and stir in the sundried tomatoes and parsley.

4. Heat the remaining olive oil in a large skillet. Sprinkle the turkey cutlets with the dried sage, salt, and pepper.

Cook the cutlets for two minutes on each side or until just cooked through.

5. Remove the turkey from the pan and add the lemon juice and capers, scraping to deglaze the pan. Continue to cook until the liquid reduces a bit.

6. Slice the turkey and serve it over the "couscous" with a drizzle of the sauce.

Easy Mediterranean Mackerel with Buckwheat Salad

Ingredients:

- 3 ounce mackerel filet
- 2 tsp. olive oil, divided
- 2 lemon slices
- ¼ c. buckwheat
- 5 olives
- 3 cherry tomatoes, halved
- 1 Tbsp. flat leaf parsley, chopped
- ½ tsp. turmeric
- Salt and pepper to taste

1. Preheat your oven's broiler and put the rack about six inches from the heat source.
2. Lightly grease a baking dish.
3. Place the mackerel filet skin-side down in the baking dish. Brush it with olive oil, sprinkle with salt and pepper, and top with the two lemon slices.
4. Put the mackerel under the broiler and cook until the fish just starts to flake, about 5 to 7 minutes.
5. Meanwhile, cook the buckwheat according to the package directions and drain it.
6. Chop the olives and add them to the buckwheat with the tomatoes and parsley. Drizzle with olive oil and stir to combine.
7. Serve the fish with the buckwheat salad on the side.

Buckwheat Pasta with Kale and Lemon

Ingredients:

- 4 ounces buckwheat noodles
- 2 handfuls baby kale, stemmed
- 1 Tbsp. capers
- 1 Tbsp. flat leaf parsley, chopped
- ½ lemon juiced
- 1 Tbsp. extra virgin olive oil

1. Prepare the buckwheat noodles per the package instructions. Drain and set aside.
2. Heat the olive oil in a large skillet. Add the kale and cook until it is just wilted, about 2-3 minutes.
3. Remove the kale and add the lemon juice and capers to the pan. Let the liquid reduce slightly (there should be some residual liquid from cooking the kale, too.)
4. Add the noodles and kale to the skillet and toss to combine with the sauce.
5. Top with the chopped parsley and serve immediately.

All of the recipes in this chapter are rich in sirtfoods and make great choices for this diet. You can feel free to experiment a bit. As long as the majority of the food you eat is sirtfood, it is perfectly acceptable to add other ingredients.

Sirtfood Snacks

I promised you a list of sirtfood snacks to close out the chapter, and here they are:

- ½ c. fresh blueberries
- ½ c. fresh sliced strawberries
- 3 ounces canned tuna packed in water with low fat mayonnaise
- 1 hardboiled egg or 1 egg white
- 1 ounce of almonds
- 1 ounce of walnuts
- 1 green apple
- ½ c. cooked buckwheat noodles or cooked buckwheat
- 1 or 2 stalks of celery
- 1 ounce dark chocolate
- 6 Medjool dates

If you want to vary your diet, you can also snack on low-sugar veggies like carrot sticks, radishes, or sugar snap peas.

Conclusion

Thank you for reading *The Sirtfood Diet*. I hope you have found the information in this book to be both useful and inspirational.

It isn't easy to find a diet that works. Many of the companies that make up the diet and fitness industry have a vested interest in making sure that you don't lose weight – at least not permanently. They want you to be dependent on them, eating their packaged foods and signing up for their support websites. They want to keep you on the diet rollercoaster, losing and gaining weight for the rest of your life.

The Sirtfood Diet is different because it uses simple, natural foods that can be found at any supermarket. These foods are not fancy, and the preparations you use to cook them are not complicated. Of course, you can feel free to experiment with the recipes in this book and find ways to make them different. Many of the ingredients can be easily substituted. For example, it would be very easy – and equally good for The Sirtfood Diet – to substitute a small tuna steak for the mackerel recipe, or to use dried blueberries instead of chocolate chips in the granola.

As long as the majority of your diet is composed of sirtfoods, and you drink your green juice every day, you will lose weight. The first three days are definitely going to be tough. I think it's important to be honest about that. Eating a very low calorie diet is a challenge, but it's one you are capable of meeting.

Conclusion

When it gets to be difficult, just remind yourself that it's only three days. You can survive anything for three days.

I do recommend that you check in with your doctor prior to starting The Sirtfood Diet. These foods are healthy to eat, but if you have any concerns about your blood sugar – whether you are diabetic, pre-diabetic, or even prone to low blood sugar – it is important to get your doctor on board before starting. In some instances, you may want to eat lean protein such as egg whites, tuna, or chicken breast with your green juice. Small changes like that will not impede your progress on the diet.

Remember that while it is acceptable to have red wine and dark chocolate on this diet, it is best to consume these things in limited quantities. I recommend having no more than one glass of wine per day – that's six ounces; and no more than a couple of ounces of dark chocolate per day. Many people find that having a square of dark chocolate after dinner helps signal their bodies that dinner is through and that the day's eating is done. If you have a tendency to snack late at night, you may want to keep that in mind.

The final thing I want to mention is that you should be sure to drink plenty of water while on this diet, and to get sufficient sleep. Guidelines may vary regarding how much water to drink, but a good rule of thumb is to drink at least eight cups per day. If you drink green tea, make sure to count that as only half the amount of water because of the caffeine content – in other words, eight ounces of tea counts for four ounces of your daily water requirement. The same goes for coffee.

When it comes to sleep, most adults require between seven and nine hours per night. A good way to tell how much sleep you need is to keep track of how long you sleep on the weekends when you don't need an alarm to get up. You can then set up a sleep schedule that enables you to go to bed and get up at the same time while ensuring that you get enough sleep.

Weight loss isn't easy, but it is possible – and The Sirtfood Diet can help you to achieve your goals. To get started, all you need to do is talk to your doctor and make a quick visit to the grocery store. The rest is easy.

Good luck, and happy eating!

ONE LAST THING...

If you enjoyed this book or found it useful I'd be very grateful if you'd post a short review on Amazon. Your support really does make a difference and I read all the reviews personally so I can get your feedback and make this book even better.

Thanks again for your support!

Danielle Wilder

Made in the USA
Monee, IL
17 January 2020